Diet recommendations for TCM - Liver - Blood stagnation

Please check these recommendations always with a nutrition consultant, therapist, doctor or dietician. The recipes and the list of ingredients are supporting the conventional medical therapy.
The calorie disclosures of fresh ingredients (fruit and vegetables) vary according to quality and time of harvest. The contents were checked by a dietician and a nutrition consultant for the Traditional Chinese Medicine (TCM).

Author:
©2019 Josef Miligui
www.ebns.at

AF187947

Source:
The lists are created from the EBNS database for nutritional counseling. The database is used by dietitians, therapists and doctors for advising the patient / client.

Literature:
The specialist literature and the training documents of the German and Austrian dietary and traditional Chinese medicine serve as a knowledge base. We have used the documents as a basis of knowledge, adapted it to our experience and completed them.
http://di-book.com

Production and publishing:
BoD – Books on Demand, Norderstedt
ISBN: 9783746088952

Diet recommendations for TCM - Liver - Blood stagnation

1   Treatment strategy

Move liver Qi, move blood, regulate.
Hot NO, cold NO, sour and bitterly warm LITTLE, everything else YES
(especially neutral and refreshing).

2   Avoid

Everything that weakens spleen and blood, salty, bitter-drying, pork,
lamb, grilled, spicy hot spices, animal fats, indigestible,
consistent: alcohol, denatured, artificial flavors, sweetener.

3   Breakfast

	kkal. per serving
Carrot soup	104
Celery soup	101
Champignon soup with red wine	269
Hearty winter breakfast	678

4   Snack

5   Lunch

6 Afternoon

7 Dinner

8 Any time

9 Recipes

(rec.) = You can use more.
(little) = You should use less than specified
(omit) = omit.

9.1 8 treasures of rice

Strengthens kidney and bladder, builds up Qi, strengthens the spleen, repels moisture, reduces internal heat, prevents cancer, builds heart, calms nerves.
Cooking time approx. 1 hour
Calories p. portion: 223
4 portions

Quantity of ingredients:
Lily bulbs 1 table spoon / 5g. () - cool - sweet, bitter .... *
Longane 1 table spoon / 5g. (yes) - warm - sweet .... *
King Solomon's-seal 1 table spoon / 5g. () - neutral - sweet, bitter .... *
Yam root, yam root tuber 1 table spoon / 5g. () - neutral - sweet .... *
Coix (seeds) YiYi Ren 1 table spoon / 5g. (rec.) - cool - sweet, neutral .... *
Rice wild (nature rice) 1 1/2 cups / 240g. (yes) - neutral - sweet, bitter..... metal
Water 8-10 cups / 800g. (yes) - cool - salty..earth

Cooking instructions:
Each one 1 tbsp: Bai He, Longan, Yu Zhu, Da Zao, Shan Yao, Lian Mi, Yi Yi Ren, Qian Shi
Add hot water and soak for about 30 minutes. Then add 1 - 2 cups of rice (normal) and simmer for 1/2 to 1 hour until the rice is very soft. Or: Cook for about 3 hours with the herbs a congee. Then the herbs do not have to be soaked.

9.2 Apple sauce with raisins

Nourishes fluids, reduces stomach heat, strengthens spleen, harmonizes stomach, moisturizes, relaxes, builds up Qi.
Cooking time approx. 25 min
Calories p. portion: 74
10 portions
Allergens: O

Quantity of ingredients:
Apple (sweet) 2,2 lbs / 1000g. (rec.) - cool - sweet, sour ....earth
Water 1/2 cup / 100g. (yes) - cool - salty..earth
Raisins 1/8 lbs - 2oz / 50g. (yes) - warm - sweet......................................earth

Cooking instructions:
Wash, peel and quarter the apples and remove the core. Put the apples with the water in a pot. Wash the raisins with hot water and add them. Cook at low heat for about 10 minutes, then allow to cool. For children up to 10 months, mash in the blender finely. For the larger ones, crush with the potato steamer. Fill and seal in a freezer or empty yoghurt jug. Close the yoghurt jug. Freeze in the shock freezer.
If necessary, thaw at room temperature for about 6 hours. (Lasting about 4 months).
The fruit mousse is intended as dessert or intermediate meal. It has an anti-digestive effect. In case of diarrhea give better banana.

9.3   Basic recipe for a chicken broth worming

Strengthens Qi and blood, is very warm.
Cooking time approx. 2-3 hours
Calories p. portion: 90
9 portions
Allergens: L

Quantity of ingredients:
Chicken meat 1/2 piece / 600g. (yes) - warm - sweet .... wood
Carrot 2 pieces / 150g. (yes) - neutral - sweet ....earth
Leek 1 stick / 45g. (rec.) - warm - acrid .... metal
Celery root 1 piece / 500g. (rec.) - cool - sweet...earth
Ginger fresh 2 slices / 2g. (little) - warm - acrid .... metal
Juniper berry 1 teaspoon / 3g. (little) - warm - sweet, acrid, bitter................fire
Bay leaf 3 pieces / 2g. () - warm - acrid.. metal
Water 4 cup / 900g. (yes) - cool - salty...earth

Cooking instructions:
Remove chicken parts from fat. Place chicken pieces in a saucepan with hot water and heat till it boils briefly, skimming any resulting foam. Add coarsely chopped vegetables and all spices and cook over medium heat for 2 to 3 hours. Strain the finished soup. Throw away vegetables and bones.
Tip: If you want to use the meat as a soup insert, take out after 45 minutes and return only the bones in the soup.
Refrigerate for later use.

9.4   Basmati rice + Zucchini tofu dish

Converts mucus, reduces heat, builds up Qi, nourishes fluids, harmonizes spleen and stomach, forces Lungen Qi.
Cooking time approx. 20 min
Calories p. portion: 146
4 portions
Allergens: E

Quantity of ingredients:
Soy Tofu 5/8 lbs - 8oz / 250g. (rec.) - cool - sweet....................................earth
Olive oil 2 table spoons / 6g. (little) - cool - sweet ....earth
Coriander 1/2 teaspoon / 4g. (rec.) - warm - acrid....................................metal
Ginger fresh 1/2 teaspoon / 4g. (little) - warm - acrid ....metal
Rice Basmati 1/2 cup / 60g. (yes) - neutral - sweet.................................metal
Water 3 cups / 200g. (yes) - cool - salty..earth
Zucchini 1 piece / 700g. (rec.) - cool - sweet..earth

Cooking instructions:
Cut tofu cubes and marinate with olive oil, tamari, crushed coriander and ginger. Leave at least 1 hour.

Cook Basmati rice with the water. You can season with onion and cardamom.
Roast zucchini and tofu in pan in the hot oil for approx. 5-7 min.
Serve rice and tofu on a plate.
Add the parsley.

Can also be used as a salad for the home and on the go.

9.5   Boiled fillet with potatoebiscuits (Austrian classic Tafelspitz)

Strengthens spleen Qi, strengthens blood and Qi, moisturizes, relaxes, builds up Qi, spreads, forces Qi, forces spleen, relieves inflammation, moisturizes.
Cooking time approx. 3 hours
Calories p. portion: 454
8 portions
Allergens: L

Quantity of ingredients:
Onion white 1 piece / 50g. (yes) - warm - acrid .... metal
Corn germ oil 1 table spoon / 10g. () - neutral - sweet .... earth
Water 32 cup - 1 gallon / 0g. (yes) - cool - salty .... earth
Beef meat 5,4 lbs - 70oz cap of rump / 1800g. (yes) - warm - sweet .... earth
Beef meatbones 4n slices with bone marrow / 0g. (yes) - warm - sweet.... earth
Salt 1 pinch / 0,5g. (little) - cold - salty .... water
Peppercorns 15 pieces / 0g. (yes) - warm - acrid....................................... metal
Parsnip 1 piece / 0g. (rec.) - cool - bitter .... fire
Carrot 2 pieces / 0g. (yes) - neutral - sweet .... earth
Celery root 1 slice / 0g. (rec.) - cool - sweet.. earth
Parsley root 2 pieces / 0g. () - cool - sweet.. earth
Leek 1/2 stick / 0g. (rec.) - warm - acrid .... metal
Chives 1 table spoon (chopped) / 7g. (rec.) - warm - acrid........................ metal
Potato 2,2 lbs / 1000g. (rec.) - neutral - sweet .... earth
Sunflower oil 2 table spoons / 20g. (little) - cool - sweet .... earth
Salt 1 pinch / 0,5g. (little) - cold - salty .... water

Cooking instructions:
Halve the onions, but do not peel. Brown onions in a pan with fat on the cut surfaces very dark. Wash meat and bones briefly with warm water, drain.

Heat the water till it boils, put in meat and cook gently. Always scoop up rising foam. As soon as no more foam rises, add peppercorns and the onion. Clean and cut root and leeks and add after about two and a half hours cooking time. Simmer for another half hour.

Remove boiled beef from the soup, pour through a sieve and season with salt. Cut roots into bite-sized pieces. Add the soup together with the marrow bones and leave it under the boiling point. Cut the boiled beef into finger-thick slices against the grain, place in the soup, heat again, sprinkle with a little chives.

In addition, cook and peel the potatoes in salted water. Stomp roughly or cut finely. Fry in a pan with the oil crispy.

9.6   Carp soup

Nourishing and slightly warming, strengthens the middle and the lower heater, removes moisture.
Cooking time approx. 2 hours
Calories p. portion: 166
6 portions
Allergens: DO

Quantity of ingredients:

Carp 1,1 lbs / 500g. (rec.) - neutral - salty .... water
Salt 1 pinch / 1g. (little) - cold - salty .... water
Vinegar (Apple vinegar) 1 teaspoon / 3g. (little) - warm - sour, bitter .... wood
Thyme 1 Twig / 3g. (little) - warm - bitter .... *
Juniper berry 8 pieces / 3g. (little) - warm - sweet, acrid, bitter .... fire
Carrot 2 pieces / 200g. (yes) - neutral - sweet .... earth
Leek 1 piece / 200g. (rec.) - warm - acrid .... metal
Onion white 1 piece / 60g. (yes) - warm - acrid .... metal
Ginger fresh 1/2 teaspoon / 2g. (little) - warm - acrid .... metal
Bay leaf 3 leaves / 1g. () - warm - acrid .... metal
White wine 1/2 cup / 125g. (little) - cool - sweet, bitter, acrid .... wood
Basil 3 leaves / 1g. (yes) - warm - acrid, bitter .... fire
Water 4 cup / 800g. (yes) - cool - salty .... earth

Cooking instructions:

Preparation: When shopping at the fishmonger, remove the fillets from a medium-sized, whole carp and also pack the fish head, spine with bones and tail.

Cut the fillets into 1 cm cubes; salt and set aside.

Place fish head, backbone and tail of carp in plenty of cold water; heat till it boils and scoop the foam; add a dash of vinegar, a fresh sprig of thyme, juniper berries; Add carrot, a piece of leek and chopped onion; add a thick slice of ginger, some peppercorns, 1 bay leaf, salt; simmer for about 1 1/2 hours and pour the stock through a sieve.

Put the carp pieces in a saucepan; pour a shot of white wine; Add rose paprika, basil leaves, finely ground carrots, dried thyme and the stock and warm; Boil the ingredients for about 5 minutes until the fish pieces are cooked.

Variants: Thicken the soup with Kuzu or mashed potatoes.
This fits: baguette and dry white wine.

9.7 Carrot soup

Strengthens spleen and liver, regulates Qi flow, moisturizes, relaxes, builds up Qi, spreads, scatters and move Qi, reduces cold-evil, softens knots, build up organs, feeds muscles, spreads, nourishes blood and liver, harmonizes liver and spleen.

Cooking time approx. 30 min
Calories p. portion: 105
4 portions
Allergens: O

Quantity of ingredients:

Carrot 1,1 lbs / 500g. (yes) - neutral - sweet .... earth
Pepper (ground) 1 pinch / 0,5g. () - warm - acrid .... metal
Nutmeg 1 pinch / 1g. (rec.) - warm - acrid .... metal
Salt 1 pinch / 1g. (little) - cold - salty .... water
White wine 1/2 cup / 125g. (little) - cool - sweet, bitter, acrid .... wood
Orange juice Alternatively for wine / 0g. (omit) - cold - sour, sweet .... wood
Parsley 2 table spoons / 10g. (little) - warm - bitter .... wood
Thyme dried Alternative to rose paprika / 0g. () - warm - bitter .... metal
Pine nuts 1 table spoon / 15g. (rec.) - neutral - sweet .... earth
Sunflower seeds Alternatively to pine nuts / 0g. (rec.) - neutral - sweet ..... earth
Water 2 cup / 450g. (yes) - cool - salty .... earth

Cooking instructions:

Place peeled large cut carrot pieces in hot water; cook and then puree;
season with ground pepper, a little nutmeg,
a pinch of salt; add a dash of white wine and simmer for a few minutes
or season with orange juice; Add parsley as desired; stir in some rose
paprika or fresh thyme; sprinkle with roasted pine nuts or sunflower
seeds before serving.

9.8 Celery soup

Refreshing, builds up fluids and Qi.
Cooking time approx. 45 min
Calories p. portion: 101
4 portions
Allergens: ACGL

Quantity of ingredients:

Water 2 cup / 500g. (yes) - cool - salty .... earth
Butter organic 1 table spoon / 15g. (yes) - neutral - sweet .... earth
Nutmeg 1 pinch / 1g. (rec.) - warm - acrid .... metal
Salt 1 pinch / 1g. (little) - cold - salty .... water
Spelled wholemeal flour 2-3 teaspoons / 25g. (yes) - neutral - sweet .... wood
Celery root 1 piece / 500g. (rec.) - cool - sweet .... earth
Chicken egg 1 piece / 55g. (rec.) - neutral - sweet .... earth
Cream sour 10% 2 table spoons / 25g. (little) - neutral - sweet .... earth
Celery sticks 2 table spoons / 20g. (rec.) - cool - sweet .... earth
Pepper (ground) 1 pinch / 0,5g. () - warm - acrid .... metal

Cooking instructions:

In a hot saucepan, melt 1 tbsp butter; add a pinch of nutmeg, a pinch of salt, 1/2 cup wholegrain spelled flour (finely ground as fresh as possible) and stir to a sweat while stirring; add 1/2 liter of hot water gradually; add 1 large finely chopped celery tuber; cook for about 35 minutes and then puree; mix 1 egg yolk with 1 cup of cream; in the hot - no longer boiling! - soup vigorously; add some celery leaves finely chopped; with pepper, salt to taste.

9.9 Champignon soup with red wine

Nourishes blood, builds up Qi, passes downwardly, nourishes blood and liver, directs heat down, nourishes mid-Qi, nourishes Yin and blood.
Cooking time approx. 15 min
Calories p. portion: 269
2 portions
Allergens: CGNO

Quantity of ingredients:
Sesame oil 2 table spoons / 20g. (little) - cool - sweet ....earth
Champignon 1 1/2 cups / 250g. (rec.) - cool - sweet...............................earth
Pepper (ground) 1 pinch / 0,2g. () - warm - acrid .... metal
Salt 1 pinch / 1g. (little) - cold - salty .... water
Sour cream 15% fat 2 table spoons / 20g. (rec.) - cool - sour .... wood
Red wine 2oz / 125g. (little) - warm - bitter...fire
Sugar cane sugar 1 pinch / 1g. (rec.) - cool - sweet................................earth
Chicken yolk 2 pieces / 40g. (little) - neutral - sweet ....earth
Nutmeg 1 pinch / 0,3g. (rec.) - warm - acrid.. metal
Parsley 2 table spoons (chopped) / 20g. (little) - warm - bitter .... wood

Cooking instructions:
Sauté briefly fry sliced mushrooms in sesame oil in a hot pot. Add pepper, salt, plenty of sour cream, hot water, a good shot of red wine; simmer for a few minutes; add a pinch of whole cane sugar, 1 egg yolk, nutmeg; season with salt; stir in fresh parsley.

9.10 Chicory salad with tangerine

Nourishing builds up fluids, in the absence of blood and lack of heart and liver fluids, emits moist heat down. Not
with middle-Qi deficiency.
Cooking time approx. 10 min
Calories p. portion: 257
3 portions
Allergens: AGNO

Quantity of ingredients:

Tangerine 4 pieces / 300g. (yes) - cool - sweet, sour .... wood
Chicory 2-3 pieces / 300g. (rec.) - cool - sweet, bitter .... fire
Sesame oil 2 table spoons / 18g. (little) - cool - sweet .... earth
Pepper (ground) 1 pinch / 0,5g. () - warm - acrid .... metal
Salt 1 pinch / 1g. (little) - cold - salty .... water
Vinegar Aceto Balsamico 2 teaspoons / 6g. () - warm - sour, bitter   wood
Lemon 1/2 piece / 25g. (omit) - cold - sour .... wood
Orange 1/2 piece / 70g. (omit) - cold - sour, sweet .... wood
Orange jam 1 teaspoon / 4g. () - cool - sour, sweet .... wood
Cream, sweet 30% 1 table spoon / 10g. (yes) - neutral - sweet .... earth
White bread (wheat bread) 6 slices / 120g. (yes) - cool - sweet .... wood

Cooking instructions:

Peel tangerines and cut into bite-sized pieces; Cut chicory roughly and mix well.

Dressing: sesame oil, pepper, salt, raspberry vinegar or balsamic vinegar, a little lemon or orange juice, rose paprika, orange marmalade or, alternatively, another jam, stir well. Give a little sweet cream over the salad and let it pass briefly.

9.11 Clear soup from goose

Forces spleen, stomach and lungs, relieves weakness, forces Qi, calms the stomach, gets Qi moving, directs upwards, strengthens spleen and liver, regulates Qi flow, moisturizes, relaxes, builds up Qi, spreads.
Cooking time approx. 2-3 hours
Calories p. portion: 334
6 portions

Quantity of ingredients:

Goose parts 1,1 lbs / 500g. (rec.) - neutral - sweet .... metal
Carrot 1 piece / 100g. (yes) - neutral - sweet .... earth
Onion (shallot) 1 piece / 25g. (yes) - warm - acrid, sweet .... metal
Leek 1 piece / 250g. (rec.) - warm - acrid .... metal
Parsley 1 Twig / 4g. (little) - warm - bitter .... wood
Lovage 1 Twig / 4g. (yes) - warm - acrid, bitter .... metal
Water 4 cup / 1000g. (yes) - cool - salty .... earth
Salt 1 pinch / 0,5g. (little) - cold - salty .... water

Cooking instructions:

Simmer goose pieces with vegetables and herbs for 2-3 hours. Sift through a fine cloth and cool. Degrease and store in the refrigerator.

9.12 Creamy potatoes with cauliflower

Forces Qi, forces spleen, relieves inflammation, moisturizes, relaxes, builds up Qi, spreads, nourishes lung Yin,
produces humors, cools inner heat, strengthens Qi and kidney Jing, harmonizes liver and spleen, forces eyesight.
Cooking time approx. 30 min
Calories p. portion: 332
1 portion
Allergens: CG

Quantity of ingredients:
Potato 3/8 lbs - 6oz / 150g. (rec.) - neutral - sweet ....earth
Cauliflower 1/8 lbs - 2oz / 50g. (rec.) - cool - sweet ....earth
Cow's milk (3.5% fat) 3 table spoons / 30g. (little) - neutral - sweet ....earth
Cream, sweet 30% 1 table spoon / 10g. (yes) - neutral - sweet.................earth
Butter organic 1 teaspoon / 10g. (yes) - neutral - sweet............................earth
Parsley 1 teaspoon / 3g. (little) - warm - bitter... wood
Chicken yolk 1 piece / 25g. (little) - neutral - sweet ....earth

Cooking instructions:
Wash the potatoes under running water, thoroughly wash the cauliflower in stagnant water.
Divide the cauliflower florets into small buds, cut the stems into pieces about 1 cm in size.
Peel the potatoes and cut into 2 cm cubes.
Heat the milk with the cream in a saucepan, add the potatoes and the cauliflower. Cook on low heat for about 15 minutes.
Put the vegetables in a plate, add the butter, the chopped parsley and the egg yolk and lightly knead and mix everything with a fork.

9.13 Decoction TCM liver-kidney1

Lowers liver yang, nourishes kidney-yin and liver-yin, tonifies the blood.
Cooking time approx. 20min.
Calories p. portion: 24
5 portions
Allergens: NO

Quantity of ingredients:
Pine nuts 9g. / 9g. (rec.) - neutral - sweet ....earth
Sesame, white 9g. / 9g. () - neutral - sweet...earth
Bocksdorn fruits (Lycii, goji berry dried 9g. / 9g. (yes) - cool - sweet, sour wood
Water 4 cup / 1000g. (yes) - cool - salty..earth

Cooking instructions:
After soaking, the herbs are cooked in a closed pot. First, the herbs are brought to a boil over high heat. Then the heat is reduced and slowly simmered for 20 min. The lid should not be removed often during the cooking process, as otherwise important ingredients can escape

After 20 minutes of cooking, the first decoction is done. Then strain the liquid through a sieve and collect in a container. This is the medicine-Sud 1.

Re-pour the herb mixture with water so that the herbs are in the water (about 1/2 liter) and simmer for 30 minutes.

Straining again, that's the remedy 2.

Pour Sud 1 and Sud 2 together and place in a sterile bottle and cap.

9.14 Hearty winter breakfast

Forces Qi and Yang, strengthens the body's defenses and warms up, helps with Qi and Yang emptiness.
Cooking time approx. 20 min
Calories p. portion: 678
1 portion
Allergens: ACEG

Quantity of ingredients:
Oat meal 1 cup / 120g. (yes) - warm - sweet...metal
Ginger fresh 1/2 teaspoon / 1g. (little) - warm - acrid ....metal
Salt 1 pinch / 1g. (little) - cold - salty ....water
Onion (spring onion) 2 pieces / 40g. (rec.) - warm - acrid ....metal
Chicken egg 1 piece / 55g. (rec.) - neutral - sweet.....................................earth
Butter organic 1 table spoon / 15g. (yes) - neutral - sweet.......................earth
Soy sauce 1 dash / 3g. (little) - cold - salty...water

Cooking instructions:
Soak oatmeal overnight. Boil in the morning with a little ginger, salt and a spring onion or leek and then let it swell until the porridge is soft. Before serving, add a whole egg to the porridge, add the butter and season to taste with a little soy sauce.

Recommendation: Especially suitable for the cold season.

9.15 Kohlrabi in chervil sauce with potatoes

Forces Qi, forces spleen, relieves inflammation, relaxes, spreads, moves Qi and blood, diuretic, strengthens spleen and liver, regulates Qi flow, cools heat, reduces internal wind and moisture, dissolves stagnation, directs upwards.
Cooking time approx. 1 hour
Calories p. portion: 188
4 portions
Allergens: GL

Quantity of ingredients:
Potato 6 pieces / 450g. (rec.) - neutral - sweet...earth
Basic recipe for a vegetable soup (nutritious) 1 cup / 300g. () - neutral - *....... *
Potato 1/4 lbs - 4oz / 100g. (rec.) - neutral - sweet ....earth
Nutmeg 1 pinch / 0,2g. (rec.) - warm - acrid.. metal
Lemon peel 1/2 teaspoon / 2g. (rec.) - cool - bitter..fire
Ginger fresh 1/2 teaspoon / 2g. (little) - warm - acrid .... metal
Lovage 1/2 teaspoon / 2g. (yes) - warm - acrid, bitter .... metal
Kohlrabi 3/4 lbs / 300g. (rec.) - neutral - acrid, sweet................................earth
Salt 1 pinch / 1g. (little) - cold - salty .... water
Pepper (ground) 1 pinch / 0,2g. () - warm - acrid .... metal
Sour cream 15% fat 3 table spoons / 30g. (rec.) - cool - sour .... wood
Chervil dried 1 Bunch / 80g. () - warm - sweet .... *

Cooking instructions:
Boil the potatoes in salted water.
Bring half of the vegetable stock to boil. Add the diced potatoes, nutmeg, lemon zest, ginger and lovage. Cover the potatoes and cook for about 10 minutes until soft and puree them with a blender until they are smooth.
Bring remaining vegetable stock to boil. Cut kohlrabi into cubes and add, cover and cook for about 8 minutes. Stir in the potato sauce and heat everything briefly.
Puree with the mixing stick chervil and sour cream. Mix the chervil cream with the kohlrabi vegetables.
Serve with the cooked, peeled potatoes.

9.16 Millet with blackberries

Keeps fluids, moisturizes lungs, tonifies blood, cools blood, detoxifies, preserves the fluids, contracts, strengthens spleen and kidney, diuretic, strengthens middle heater, moisturizes.
Cooking time approx. 30 min
Calories p. portion: 348
? portions
Allergens: H

Quantity of ingredients:
Water 1 1/2 cups / 240g. (yes) - cool - salty...earth
Millet 1 cup / 100g. (rec.) - cool - sweet, salty ....earth
Walnuts 2 table spoons (grounded) / 18g. (yes) - warm - sweet ....earth
Linseed oil 1 table spoon / 10g. (little) - neutral - sweet ....earth
Honey 2 table spoons / 20g. (omit) - cold - sweet ....earth
Ginger fresh 1/2 teaspoon (grated) / 1g. (little) - warm - acrid..................metal
Salt 1 pinch / 0,5g. (little) - cold - salty ....water
Blackberry´s 5/8 oz / 200g. (yes) - neutral - sweet, sour..........................wood
Acerola fruit nectar or powder 1 teaspoon / 2g. () - warm - sour ....wood
Lemon Balm (fresh) 2-4 leaves / 1g. () - cool - sour.................................metal

Cooking instructions:
Simmer the millet for 5 min and let it swell for another 30 min.
Add the walnuts and cover the millet. Simmer on a low heat until soft.
Cook for 10-15 minutes. Season the millet with honey, fresh grated ginger, salt and acerola and leave to soak for another 10 minutes. In the meantime, wash blackberries and finely chop lemon balm. Mix millet with blackberries and lemon balm and serve warm.

Tip: The millet can be well pre-cooked in the evening. In the morning just warm briefly, mix with blackberries and lemon balm and serve.

9.17 Millet with egg and butter

Forces blood, Yin and Jing, nourishes Yin, moisturizes in case of internal dryness, forces blood, forces spleen, calms nerves and stomach, strengthens spleen and kidney, diuretic, strengthens Qi and kidney Jing, moisturizes, relaxes, builds up Qi, spreads
Cooking time approx. 25 min
Calories p. portion: 338
2 portions
Allergens: CG

Quantity of ingredients:
Millet 1 cup / 100g. (rec.) - cool - sweet, salty ....earth
Ginger fresh 1/2 teaspoon / 1g. (little) - warm - acrid .... metal
Salt 1 pinch / 0,5g. (little) - cold - salty .... water
Parsley 2 table spoons / 16g. (little) - warm - bitter.................................. wood
Pepper powder (hot) 1 pinch / 1g. () - warm - bitter....................................fire
Chicken egg 2 pieces / 100g. (rec.) - neutral - sweet.................................earth
Butter organic 2 table spoons / 20g. (yes) - neutral - sweet ....earth
Nutmeg 1 pinch / 0,2g. (rec.) - warm - acrid...metal
Water 1 1/2 cups / 200g. (yes) - cool - salty..earth

Cooking instructions:
Simmer the millet with the ginger and nutmeg in the water for 5 min.
and let it swell for another 30 min.
Cook and peel 1 soft egg per person; pile up the millet on plates and
place 1 egg each in a hollow in the millet mountain; Put butter flakes
over it. Sprinkle with chopped parsley and the rose paprika.

9.18 Nettle-chard soup

Drains moisture down, strengthens blood, cools liver heat.
Cooking time approx. 30 min
Calories p. portion: 52
4 portions

Quantity of ingredients:
Nettles 1 handful / 10g. () - neutral - bitter.. wood
Chard 1 lbs / 500g. (rec.) - cool - bitter, sweet ....earth
Salt 1 pinch / 1g. (little) - cold - salty .... water
Water 2 cup / 400g. (yes) - cool - salty..earth
Olive oil 1 table spoon / 10g. (little) - cool - sweet ....earth
Pepper (ground) 1 pinch / 0,5g. () - warm - acrid .... metal

Cooking instructions:
Heat the oil in a saucepan, add the washed and finely chopped Swiss
chard. Salt and let simmer for 10 minutes. Add the chopped nettles and
cook for another 10 minutes. Add pepper and puree.

9.19 Oat flakes with aromatic spices

Nourishes fluids, reduces stomach heat, forces spleen, produces essence, harmonizes stomach, forces Qi, strengthens kidney Qi, essence and brain, moisturizes, relaxes, spreads.
Cooking time approx. 25 min
Calories p. portion: 280
3 portions
Allergens: AH

Quantity of ingredients:
Oat flakes (whole grain) 1 cup / 125g. (yes) - warm - sweet .... metal
Walnuts 1 table spoon / 15g. (yes) - warm - sweet .... earth
Hazelnuts 1 table spoon / 15g. (rec.) - neutral - sweet .... earth
Water 1 1/2 cups / 240g. (yes) - cool - salty .... earth
Wakame 1 inch / 2g. (rec.) - cold - salty .... water
Apple (sweet) 1 piece / 220g. (rec.) - cool - sweet, sour .... earth
Cardamom 3-4 capsules / 2g. () - warm - acrid .... metal
Lemon Balm (fresh) 3-4 leaves / 3g. () - cool - sour .... metal
Acerola fruit nectar or powder 1 teaspoon / 2g. () - warm - sour .... wood

Cooking instructions:
Roast oatmeal and nuts. Add hot water. Add cardamom, wakame and cook for 20 min. Add grated apple, acerola and lemon herb.

9.20 Potatoes with wild garlic-curd cheese

Forces Qi, forces spleen, relieves inflammation, nourishes blood and Yi, forces Zang-organs, forces stomach and intestines, harmonizes Qi, relieves alcohol poisoning, moisturizes lungs, gets Qi moving.
Cooking time approx. 20 min
Calories p. portion: 254
2 portions
Allergens: G

Quantity of ingredients:
Potato 3/4 lbs / 300g. (rec.) - neutral - sweet .... earth
Salt 1 pinch / 0,1g. (little) - cold - salty .... water
Wild garlic (garlic spinach) 2 handful / 30g. () - warm - sweet, little acrid .. metal
Curd cheese 20% 5/8 lbs - 8oz / 250g. (yes) - cool - sour........................ wood
Yogurt (natural, 1.5% fat) 2 table spoons / 20g. (omit) - cool - sour .... wood
Salt 1 pinch / 1g. (little) - cold - salty .... water

Cooking instructions:
Cook potatoes in salted water and peel.
Wash he wild garlic leaves and carefully dried and cut into fine strips.
Mix the cottage cheese, yogurt and salt and mix in the chopped wild garlic pieces. Serve with the potatoes.
In the season in which no wild garlic grows the wild garlic pesto can be used.

9.21 Pumpkin soup

Forces lungs and spleen, diuretic, forces Qi, protects liver, forces Qi, forces spleen, relieves inflammation, moisturizes, relaxes, builds up Qi, spreads, strengthens spleen and liver, regulates Qi flow, moisturizes, relaxes, builds up Qi, spreads.
Cooking time approx. 1 hour
Calories p. portion: 105
3 portions

Quantity of ingredients:
Pumpkin 3/4 lbs / 300g. (yes) - warm - sweet ....earth
Carrot 2 pieces / 100g. (yes) - neutral - sweet ....earth
Potato 2 pieces / 120g. (rec.) - neutral - sweet...earth
Olive oil 1 table spoon / 10g. (little) - cool - sweet....................................earth
Onion white 1 piece / 50g. (yes) - warm - acrid ....metal
Water 1 cup / 120g. (yes) - cool - salty...earth
Parsley 1 table spoon / 7g. (little) - warm - bitter..................................... wood
Anise (Common Fennel) 1 pinch / 1g. (yes) - warm - acrid ....earth
Salt 1 pinch / 1g. (little) - cold - salty .... water

Cooking instructions:
Add the olive oil to the pan, add the diced pumpkin, diced carrots and potatoes. Roast them shortly, add the finely chopped onion, fill with water, add enough water to cover the vegetables at least 3 finger-widths. Boil at low heat.

Season with sea salt, add small cutted parsley, a pinch of anise (little). Allow to simmer for about 35 minutes. Then purée the soup and add some water, depending on the consistency of the soup.

9.22 Quick zucchini soup

Reduces mucus, preserves the fluids, cools liver fire, forces stomach Qi.
Cooking time approx. 10 min
Calories p. portion: 42
4 portions

Quantity of ingredients:
Zucchini 2-3 pieces / 500g. (rec.) - cool - sweet..earth
Onion white 1 piece / 50g. (yes) - warm - acrid......................................metal
Corn germ oil 2 table spoons / 6g. () - neutral - sweet ....earth
Parsley 1 table spoon / 7g. (little) - warm - bitter......................................wood
Chives 1 teaspoon / 3g. (rec.) - warm - acrid ....metal
Water 2 cup / 400g. (yes) - cool - salty...earth

Cooking instructions:
Fry chopped onion in oil. Add sliced zucchini and sauté well. Pour with water. Chop parsley and chives, add and puree everything.

9.23 Radish with horseradish

Slightly refreshing and moisturizing, dissolves stagnation, nourishes blood and liver, harmonizes liver and spleen, forces eyesight, preserves the fluids, contracts, nourishes the lungs and spleen, distributes mucus, dissolves mucus, dissolves stagnation,
Cooking time approx. 30 min
Calories p. portion: 196
2 portions
Allergens: GNO

Quantity of ingredients:
Butter organic 1 table spoon / 8g. (yes) - neutral - sweet...........................earth
Radish (white, green…) 1/2 piece / 50g. (yes) - cool - sweet, acrid ....metal
Water 3 table spoons / 10g. (yes) - cool - salty ....earth
Lemon juice 2 table spoons / 20g. (omit) - cold - sour...............................wood
White wine 2 table spoons / 20g. (little) - cool - sweet, bitter, acrid...........wood
Pepper powder (hot) 1 pinch / 0,2g. () - warm - bitter....................................fire
Sesame oil 1 teaspoon / 3g. (little) - cool - sweet......................................earth
Horseradish 2 table spoons / 20g. (little) - neutral - sweet, little acrid ....metal
Salt 1 pinch / 0,5g. (little) - cold - salty ....water
Parsley 1 Bunch (chopped) / 80g. (little) - warm - bitter ....wood
Rice long grain rice 1/2 cup / 60g. (yes) - neutral - sweet ....metal
Water 3 cups / 300g. (yes) - cool - salty...earth
Salt 1 pinch / 0,5g. (little) - cold - salty ....water

Cooking instructions:
In a hot pan melt the butter, sautéed into stripes cut radish. Add cold water, lemon juice, white wine, a pinch of rose paprika and stir in the sesame oil; with 2 - 3 tablespoons fresh grated horseradish (alternatively 1 teaspoon from the glass), salt to taste; Sprinkle with chopped parsley.

Place the rice with the water, salt and cook for about 15 minutes.

9.24 Rice congee with chicken liver and buckthorn fruit

Warms the stomach and spleen, harmonizes the intestine, forces Qi, reduces moisture, nourishes liver-blood, nourishes and forces liver, forces kidney, forces blood, makes eyes clear.
Cooking time approx. 3 hours
Calories p. portion: 176
3 portions
Allergens: EO

Quantity of ingredients:
Basic recipe for a rice soup (Congee) 5 cups / 800g. (yes) - neutral - sweet ... *
Chicken liver 1/2 cup / 60g. (little) - warm - sweet, bitter..............................earth
Bocksdorn fruits (Lycii, goji berry dried 1/2 cup / 60g. (yes) - cool - .... wood
Soy sauce 1 dash / 3g. (little) - cold - salty.. water

Cooking instructions:
Cook basic recipe for rice congee with the chicken liver and wolfberry fruits; Season with soy sauce.

9.25 Rice with parsnips

Regulates Qi, dries out, passes downwardly, warms the stomach and spleen, harmonizes the intestine, forces Qi, reduces moisture.
moisturizes, relaxes, builds up Qi, spreads. distributes mucus, activates Wei Qi, forces Qi.
Cooking time approx. 45 min
Calories p. portion: 206
3 portions

Quantity of ingredients:
Rice variety any 1 cup / 120g. (yes) - warm - sweet.............................metal
Water 1 1/2 cups / 200g. (yes) - cool - salty....................................earth
Salt 1 pinch / 1g. (little) - cold - salty ....water
Parsnip 3-4 pieces / 450g. (rec.) - cool - bitter ....fire
Olive oil 1 table spoon / 10g. (little) - cool - sweet...........................earth
Sage 1 teaspoon / 3g. (rec.) - cool - bitter, spicy............................fire

Cooking instructions:
Peel the parsnips and cut into slices. Fry for a short time in oil. Add the rice and fry again for a short time. Add the water and cook it at least 30 min. Sprinkle with fresh chopped sage.

9.26 Roasted millet with Celery sticks

Strengthens spleen and kidney, diuretic, brings the liver Qi in motion, cools heat, moisturizes, relaxes, builds up
Qi, spreads.
Cooking time approx. 30 min
Calories p. portion: 400
2 portions
Allergens: L

Quantity of ingredients:
Millet 1 cup / 120g. (rec.) - cool - sweet, salty ....earth
Water 1 1/2 cups / 240g. (yes) - cool - salty,,,,,,,,,, ...earth
Celery sticks 2 rods / 50g. (rec.) - cool - sweet ....earth
Water 2 table spoons / 30g. (yes) - cool - salty ....earth
Salt 1 pinch / 1g. (little) - cold - salty ....water
Sage 3-4 leaves / 2g. (rec.) - cool - bitter, spicy............................fire
Cress 1 teaspoon / 3g. (yes) - cool - sweet....................................metal

Cooking instructions:
Roast millet briefly, pour over water, heat till it boils and let stand for 20 min. to swell.

Cut celery into small pieces and mix with water, salt and fresh herbs and cook for 10 min. Add to the millet. Sprinkle fresh sage or watercress over it.

9.27 Roasted nuts

Strengthens kidney Qi, essence and brain, forces kidney, builds up essence, warms lungs, moistens the intestine, moisturizes, relaxes, builds up Qi, spreads.
Cooking time approx. 5 min
Calories p. portion: 973
2 portions
Allergens: H

Quantity of ingredients:
Hazelnuts 1/4 lbs - 4oz / 100g. (rec.) - neutral - sweet.................earth
Cashews 1/4 lbs - 4oz / 100g. (rec.) - cool - sweet......................earth
Walnuts 1/4 lbs - 4oz / 100g. (yes) - warm - sweet......................earth

Cooking instructions:
Roast nuts in a pan for about 5 minutes.

9.28 Rosemary Potatoes

Forces Qi, forces spleen, relieves inflammation, relaxes, builds up Qi, spreads.
Cooking time approx. 30 min
Calories p. portion: 188
2 portions

Quantity of ingredients:
Potato 6-8 pieces / 420g. (rec.) - neutral - sweet ....earth
Olive oil 1 table spoon / 10g. (little) - cool - sweet ....earth
Rosemary 1 teaspoon / 2g. (rec.) - warm - bitter..fire

Cooking instructions:
Cut the potatoes into half´s, apply a little olive oil on the cut surface, then salt, sprinkle 2 - 3 rosemary needles on the potatoes.
Place the potatoes on the baking tray and bake them in the preheated oven for approx. 25 minutes to 190°C/374°F.

9.29 Stew with sweet potato and leeks

Forces Qi and Yang, is very warming, harmonizes Zang-organs, gets Qi moving, passes downwardly, strengthens Qi and Kidney Jing, builds up Qi, spreads, expels Wind-Cold to the Qi-Layer.
Cooking time approx. 30 min
Calories p. portion: 316
2 portions
Allergens: GO

Quantity of ingredients:
Sweet potato 5/8 oz / 200g. (rec.) - warm - sweet.....................................earth
Leek 1/8 lbs - 2oz / 50g. (rec.) - warm - acrid..metal
Butter organic 2 table spoons / 20g. (yes) - neutral - sweet.......................earth
Nutmeg 1 pinch / 0,1g. (rec.) - warm - acrid..metal
Basic recipe for a beef soup (warming) 2 cup / 480g. () - warm - *..................*
Salt 1 pinch / 1g. (little) - cold - salty..water
Turmeric (yellow root) 1 pinch / 0,5g. (yes) - warm - bitter..............................*
Black caraway 1 pinch / 1g. () - warm - acrid, sweet.......................................*

Cooking instructions:
Peel potatoes, cut into coarse cubes and cook (not too soft) in salted water, drain. Heat the butter in a saucepan and sauté the leek. Add the soup and add the leek and the sweet potato. Season with nutmeg, turmeric, fresh herbs, crushed black cumin and salt.

9.30 Tea from celery sticks

Brings the Liver Qi in motion, cools heat, moisturizes, relaxes, builds up Qi, spreads.
Cooking time approx. 15 min
Calories p. portion: 1
4 portions
Allergens: L

Quantity of ingredients:
Celery sticks 2 table spoons (chopped) / 18g. (rec.) - cool - sweet............earth
Water 2 cup / 500g. (yes) - cool - salty..earth

Cooking instructions:
Heat the water till it boils and put it aside. Add cutted celery and cook for 10 min. to let go. Strain. Sweet to taste with honey.

9.31 Tea from rose hip

Strengthens spleen Qi.
Cooking time approx. 10 min
Calories p. portion: 2
4 portions

Quantity of ingredients:
Rose hip tea 2 table spoons / 4g. (little) - warm - sour, sweet.................. wood
Water 2 cup / 500g. (yes) - cool - salty..earth

Cooking instructions:
Heat the water till it boils and put it aside. Add rosehip and leave for 10 min. to let go. Sweet to taste with honey. Strain when pouring.

9.32 Tea from rosemary

Dries out, passes downwardly, forces heart, lung and spleen Qi, forces liver-blood, forces heart-Yin, expels spleen heat / cold moisture, strengthens spleen and kidney Yang.
Cooking time approx. 15 min
Calories p. portion: 1
4 portions

Quantity of ingredients:
Rosemary 2-4 teaspoons / 6g. (rec.) - warm - bitter.....................................fire
Water 2 cup / 500g. (yes) - cool - salty..earth

Cooking instructions:
Heat the water till it boils and put it aside. Add rosemary and 10 min. to let go. Strain. Sweet to taste with honey.

9.33 Tea from sage

Distributes mucus, passes downwardly, activates Wei Qi, forces Qi.
Cooking time approx. 15 min
Calories p. portion: 4
4 portions

Quantity of ingredients:
Sage 2 teaspoons / 6g. (rec.) - cool - bitter, spicy ....fire
Water 2 cup / 500g. (yes) - cool - salty..earth

Cooking instructions:
Heat the water till it boils and put it aside. Add sage and 10 min. to let go. Strain. Sweet to taste with honey.

9.34 Tea Green tea

Reduces internal heat, dissolves mucus, detoxifies
Cooking time approx. 10 min
Calories p. portion: 2
1 portion

Quantity of ingredients:
Green tea 1 teaspoon / 2g. (rec.) - cool - sweet, bitter ....fire
Water 1 cup / 120g. (yes) - cool - salty...earth

Cooking instructions:
For each cup you use a teaspoonful or a teabag.
Pour green tea only with 60 to 80 ° C / 140 to 176 °F hot water, otherwise it will be bitter.
If the tea has a stimulating effect, let it draw for two to three minutes. It has a calming effect for a duration of five minutes (no longer, otherwise it will be bitter!).
Another method: Pour the tea leaves with about 70 ° C / 158 °F hot water and pour the water immediately again. Then just pour hot water again. The bitter substances disappear and the tea gets a milder aroma.

9.35 Tsampa with Jam or fruit compote

Nourishes fluids, reduces stomach heat, forces spleen, produces essence, harmonizes stomach, moisturizes intestines.
Cooking time approx. 5 min
Calories p. portion: 280
1 portion
Allergens: AGO

Quantity of ingredients:
Tsampa (roasted) 3 table spoons / 30g. () - cold - sweet, little salty ....earth
Water 6-8 table spoons / 70g. (yes) - cool - salty ....earth
Butter organic 1/2 teaspoon / 2g. (yes) - neutral - sweet............................earth
Strawberry jam 1 table spoon / 7g. () - neutral - sweet, sour.................... wood
Sunflower seeds 2 teaspoons / 14g. (rec.) - neutral - sweet ....earth
Apple (sweet) 1 piece grated / 120g. (rec.) - cool - sweet, sour ....earth

Cooking instructions:
Pour Tsampa with boiling water and stir with a spoon until a porridge is formed.
Add butter, jam, sunflower seeds and grated apple.
Sweet to taste with honey, whole cane sugar, or barley malt.
Spices and herbs: fresh mint, vanilla or cocoa, anise, cinnamon

Summer: jam or compote of your choice
Winter: nuts and apple or pear

9.36 Vegetable semolina soup

Strengthens spleen and liver, regulates Qi flow, builds up Qi, dries out, passes downwardly, reduces moisture, regulates Qi.
Cooking time approx. 20 min
Calories p. portion: 199
3 portions
Allergens: AEGL

Quantity of ingredients:
Basic recipe for a vegetable soup (nutritious) 2 cup / 500g. () - neutral - *....... *
Potato 1 piece / 80g. (rec.) - neutral - sweet ....earth
Parsnip 1 piece / 180g. (rec.) - cool - bitter ....fire
Carrot 1 piece / 120g. (yes) - neutral - sweet ....earth
Celery root 3/8 lbs - 6oz / 150g. (rec.) - cool - sweet.................................earth
Kohlrabi 1/2 piece / 200g. (rec.) - neutral - acrid, sweet............................earth
Beans (green, fresh) 1/4 lbs / 100g. () - neutral - sweet ....water
Wheat semolina 2 table spoons / 24g. (little) - cool - sweet, salty .... wood
Lovage 1/2 teaspoon / 2g. (yes) - warm - acrid, bitter .... metal
Butter organic 1 table spoon / 20g. (yes) - neutral - sweet........................earth
Soy sauce 1 teaspoon / 3g. (little) - cold - salty.. water

Cooking instructions:
Worm the prepared vegetable soup; cook the vegetables in the soup softly. Spread some wheatgrass and let it swell. At the end, add lovage-green and a little butter and taste with soy sauce.

10 Effects of food

10.1 Use ingredients: recommendable

Apple (sweet)
Arrowroot
Artichoke
Asparagus (green or white)
Barley
Barley not peeled
Beef liver
Beef meat (calf)
Boletus mushroom
Broccoli
Brussels sprouts
Buckwheat
Calamari
Carp
Cashews
Cauliflower
Celery root
Celery sticks
Champignon
Chanterelle
Chard
Chicken egg
Chickpeas
Chicory
Chinese cabbage
Chives
Chlorella (fresh water)
Coconut flakes
Coconut grated
Coix (seeds) YiYi Ren
Coriander
Corn
Crucian
Elderberry blossom tee
Fig
Fig dried
Fish pieces mixed (fresh water)
Freshwater fish
Goose
Goose parts
Gourd
Grape juice red
Grape juice white
Grapes red
Green tea
Hazelnuts
Herring
Iceberg lettuce
Kohlrabi

Kombu seaweed (Saccharina japonica)
Kumquats
Leek
Lemon peel
Millet
Millet flakes
Morel (black, dried)
Morel, dried
Nutmeg
Octopus
Onion (spring onion)
Oregano dried
Oysters
Parsnip
Peanuts
Peas
Peas, green
Perch
Pigeon
Pine nuts
Pistachios
Potato
Pumpkin seeds
Rabbit
Rabbit meat
Radicchio
Red beet
Red cabbage
Reishi mushroom
Rice sweet
Romaine lettuce / lettuce salad
Rosemary
Safflower (Dyer's thistle / Hong Hua)
Saffron
Sage
Salmon
Salsify
Shark
Shiitake, dried
Sour cream (Schmand) 30% fat
Sour cream 15% fat
Soy Tofu
Soybean milk
Soybeans, black
Soybeans, yellow
Spelled grain
Spinach
Sugar candy white
Sugar cane sugar

Sugar fructose - fruit sugar
Sugar glucose - grapes sugar
Sugar Milk Sugar
Sunflower seeds
Sweet potato
Tarragon (Estragon)

Trout
Vanilla
Vanilla powder
Wakame
Zucchini

10.2 Use ingredients: yes

Adzuki beans
Almond marzipan
Almond milk
Almond puree
Amaranth
Anchovy / Sardine
Anise (Common Fennel)
Apple (sour)
Apple juice (natural cloudy)
Apricot
Apricots
Balm
Basic recipe for a rice soup (Congee)
Basil
Basil (fresh)
Beef fillet
Beef meat
Beef meatbones
Beef Oxtail pieces
Beef soup meat
Beef stomach
Berries of the season
Bitter melon
Black tea
Blackberry´s
Black-eyed peas
Blueberry
Blueberry juice
Bocksdorn fruits (Fructus Lycii, goji berry dried
Breadcrumbs (wheat bread, bread roll)
Bulgur (cereals)
Butter organic
Carrot
Carrot (Early Carrot)
Carrot juice without sugar
Chestnuts
Chicken meat
Clementines
Clove
Coconut milk
Cod
Corn Grease (Polenta)
Couscous
Cranberries

Cranberry
Cranberry
Cranberry juice
Cream 10% coffee cream
Cream, sweet 30%
Cress
Cumin (Caraway seed)
Curd cheese 20%
Curd cheese 40%
Currant (black)
Currant (red)
Currant (white)
Dates dried
Deer meat
Deer meat
Dill
Eel
Elderberries
Endive salad
Fennel tea
Fish innards
Fish remains
French beans
Fresh cheese
Goose egg
Gooseberry
Grapes white
Grass carp
Ground
Ground caraway
Guava
Hawthorn
Herbs different varieties
Herbs of Provence
Herbs various
Herbs wild
Horse meat
Lettuce
Lobster
Longane
Lovage
Mallow (Malva sylvestris) blossom tea
Marjoram
Mediterranean fish (cod, plaice, haddock, sea eel, mackerel)

Multi-grain bread (gray bread)
Mustard seeds
Oat
Oat flakes (whole grain)
Oat flour
Oat fusion (baby food)
Oat meal
Okra
Olives
Onion (shallot)
Onion read
Onion white
Oyster mushroom
Pear
Pear juice
Pepper Cayenne
Pepper white (ground)
Peppercorns
Peppers
Pheasant
Plaice
Pomegranate
Pumpkin
Quinoa
Radish (white, green, purple-red)
Radish black
Raisins
Raspberry
Raspberry dried (immature)
Rice (fragrance)
Rice (whole grain)
Rice Basmati
Rice black
Rice flour
Rice long grain rice

Rice malt
Rice noodles
Rice red
Rice round grain
Rice variety any
Rice wild (nature rice)
Rooibos tea
Rye
Rye flour
Sago (cereals)
Sauerkraut (cutted cabbage fermented)
Shrimp
Sour cherries
Sour milk cheese 20%
Spelled (Dark) bread
Spelled semolina
Spelled wholemeal flour
Spiny lobsters
Star anise
Strawberries
Strawberry Juice
Sugar brown
Tangerine
Tuna
Turkey breast meat
Turkey ham
Turmeric (yellow root)
Walnuts
Water
Water hot
White bread (wheat bread)
Whitefish
Wild boar meat
Wild strawberries
Yoghurt vanilla

10.3 Use ingredients: little

Agar agar (kelp)
Bean oil
Beef bone marrow
Beef kidney
Beer (Pils)
Beer (Top-fermented German dark beer)
Berry juice
Blueberry jam
Borage oil
Boxhorn clover seeds
Broad beans (thick beans)
Buttermilk
Caviar
Cereal coffee

Cherry
Cherry juice
Chicken liver
Chicken yolk
Cocoa
Coffee
Cooking oil
Cottage cheese
Cow's milk (1.5% fat)
Cow's milk (whole milk 3.5% fat)
Cream sour 10%
Crème fraiche cheese
Currant jam (red)
Eel smoked
Emmental cheese

Evening primrose oil
Fennel
Feta cheese
Fresh cheese with herbs
Ginger fresh
Ginger oil
Goat
Goat and sheep's milk
Goat cheese
Gorgonzola
Gouda cheese
Green spelt
Hijiki
Hyssop
Juniper berry
Kefir
Lentils
Lentils black
Lentils red
Lentils yellow
Linseed oil
Lychee
Lychee in Preserved
Manioc flour
Margarine
Margarine (diet)
Mineral water
Miso
Miso black (fermented)
Miso paste (soy bean paste)
Mozzarella
Mung bean
Mussels
Noodles (wheat) with egg
Noodles (wheat, lasagne) with egg
Noodles (wheat, ribbon noodles) with egg
Noodles (wheat, spaghetti) with egg
Noodles (whole grain) with egg
Olive oil
Papaya
Parmesan
Parsley
Peaches
Peaches (canned)

Peanut oil
Peppers (rose peppers)
Poppy
Processed cheese 12%
processed cheese 30%
Pumpkin seed oil
Quail
Quail egg
Quince
Radish horseradish
Rapeseed oil
Raspberry jam
Red wine
Rose hip tea
Sake
Salt
Seacrab
Sesame oil
Skim milk powder
Sour milk
Soy sauce
Soybean oil
Sunflower oil
Thistle oil
Thyme
Trout (smoked)
Umeboshi plums (Japanese apricots)
Vinegar (Apple vinegar)
Walnut oil
Wheat
Wheat beer
Wheat bran
Wheat bulgur
Wheat flakes
Wheat flatbread/pita bread
Wheat flour
Wheat flour whole grain
Wheat germ oil
Wheat semolina
Wheat semolina for children
Wheat/Rye/Gray-black bread with yeast
Wheatgrass juice
White beans
White wine

10.4 Do not use contra-acting foods

Aubergine
Avocado
Bamboo shoots
Banana
Banana (cooking banana)
Burdock root tea

Cantaloupe
Carambola (Star fruit)
Chili (pod or ground)
Cinnamon ground
Cinnamon sticks
Crab

Cucumber
Curry
Dandelion (young plants)
Dandelionroots tea
Garlic
Ginger powder
Grapefruit (Pomelo)
Grapefruit juice
Honey
Kiwi
Lady's mantle
Lamb bones
Lamb kidneys
Lamb liver
Lamb meat
Lamb shoulder
Lamb's lettuce
Lemon
Lemon juice
Lime
Mango
mango powder
Mold cheese
Mulberry fruit
Mullet
Mung bean sprouting

Mutton
Mutton
Orange
Orange juice
Pimento
Pineapple
Pineapple (from a can)
Pineapple juice without sugar
Plum
Pork Bacon
Pork heart
Pork knuckle
Pork liver
Pork meat
Pork skin
Pork stomach
Radish
Rhubarb
Sorrel
Sugar white
Tomato
Watermelon
Yarrow tea
Yogi tea
Yogurt (natural, 1.5% fat)
Yogurt (natural, 3.5% fat)

11 Complementary

11.1 Agrimony

Agrimonia eupatoria
Preparation: Healing tea (infusion)
Moves and regulates Liver-Qi and Gallbladder-Qi, astringent, quenches bleeding, strengthens Spleen-Qi and Stomach-Qi, transforms moisture, dissipates Moisture-Heat.
The herb contains many bitter and tannins and therefore helps as a tea in gastrointestinal diseases and liver disease. As a gargle, however, also relieves gingivitis, sore throat and coughing.
Dosage: 1-4 g of dried tea as a decoction, 1-4 ml tincture

11.2 Balm

melissa off.
Preparation: Healing tea (infusion)
Keeps the juices, pulls together, soothes Liver-fire, soothes Shen, strengthens the blood, stimulates Lungs Qi. Easily strengthening heart-

blood and liver-blood.
Active ingredients: citronellol, citral, caryophyllene, tannin and. Bitter substances, flavonoids
Dosage: Pour 3 teaspoons of cut lemon balm leaves per cup with ¼ liter of boiling water and cover for 10 minutes.

11.3 Greater celandine, nipplewort, swallowwort

Chelidonium majus, herb.
Preparation: Different effects
Moves liver-qi and blood, regulates heart-qi, lung-qi, intestinal-qi, and middle-qi. Moves stagnant body fluids, diuretic.
Active ingredients: Alaloids (similar to opium), saponins, flavonoids, aeth. Oil, carotenoids, ferments
Note: Contains alkaloids, so it is a poisonous plant; take only with the agreement of the doctor. Inhibiting tumors. Do not use in children under 12 and in pregnant women (alkaloids, belongs to the poppy family).

12 Basics of Nutrition

The basic principles of nutrition described herein are general recommendations. They are not aimed at a specific form of therapy. Recommendations concerning a therapy have priority.

12.1 Nutrition

Regular meals in a relaxed atmosphere. A warm breakfast is considered a good start into the day.
The main meals ought to be taken for lunch – supper in the early evening. Pay attention to feeling hungry or sated: don't eat too much nor remain hungry is the rule
Prepare the meals freshly from natural, regional products. Frozen, heat-conserved, industrially prepared or foodstuffs cooked in the microwave oven are rejected.
Choice of foodstuffs according to the season: more cooling food in summer, more warming food in winter.
Eat cooked food at least twice a day. Food and drinks ought to be lukewarm, never ice-cold or hot.
Raw vegetables, briefly cooked vegetables, freshly squeezed juices and mineral water are not recommended. Milk and dairy products are only included in the diet if they don't cause problems.
Don't use therapeutic recipes over a longer period without consulting your doctor or therapist.

Varied food
Enjoy the diversity of foodstuffs. Characteristics of a balanced nutrition are variety, suitable combination and a balanced quantity of rich and low energy foodstuffs (on one hand avoiding undersupply with essential nutrients and on the other hand to take to many undesirable substances).

A lot of Cereal Products - and Potatoes
Bread, pasta, rice, cereal flakes (best wholemeal) as well as potatoes contain almost no fat, but many vitamins, mineral nutrients, trace elements, roughage and secondary plant substances. These foodstuffs ought to be taken with low-fat side dishes.

Vegetables and Fruit – „Take Five" every day …
5 portions of vegetables and fruit a day, as fresh as possible, briefly cooked, or maybe one portion as a juice – ideal as a side dish to every meal as well as snack between meals: Thus a lot of vitamins, mineral nutrients as well as roughage and secondary plant substances

Daily milk and dairy products
Milk and Dairy Products every Day, once or twice per Week Fish; meat, sausages as well as eggs moderately. These foodstuffs contain valuable nutrients like calcium in the milk, iodine selenium and omega-3 fat acids in saltwater fish. Meat is favorable due to its high content of disposable iron and the vitamins B1, B6 and B12. Quantities of 300 – 600 g meat and sausage per week are sufficient. Prefer low-fat products, especially in meat- and dairy products.

Low-fat and fatty Foodstuffs
Fat supplies us with essential fat acids and fatty foodstuffs contain also fat-soluble vitamins. Fat is high in energy; therefore much fat in the food may cause overweight, possibly also cancer. Too many saturated fat acids may further a tendency for cardio-vascular diseases in the long term. Prefer vegetable oils and fats (e.g. rapeseed-, olive-, soya-oils and solid fats produced therefrom). Beware of invisible fat in meat- and dairy products, pastry and sweets as well as in fast-food and convenience foods. 70 – 90 g fat per day is sufficient.

Moderately Sugar and Salt
Take sugar and foods/drinks containing various kinds of sugar (e.g. glucose syrup) only occasionally. Use herbs and spices as well as a little salt creatively. Prefer salt containing iodine.

Plenty of Liquids
Water is absolutely essential. Drink 1-2 l liquids every day. Prefer water (with or without gas) and other low-calorie drinks. Alcoholic drinks should not be taken.

Tasty Dishes, carefully cooked
Cook the meals with as low temperatures and as short as possible, using little water and fat – this preserves the original taste, keeps the nutrients intact and prevents the production of harmful compounds.

Take time and enjoy the food
Take your Time and enjoy your Food
Eating consciously helps to eat right. The eye enjoys food, too. It's fun, invites to enjoy varied dishes and stimulates the feeling of satiety.

Watch your Weight and stay in Motion
A balanced diet and a lot of exercise and sport (30 – 60 min/day) are a healthy combination. The right weight furthers well-being and health. Thermals, directional effectiveness, digestive power

There are various criteria for judging the effectiveness of herbs and foodstuffs.

The use of certain herbs and ingredients is based on observations of the effects on the body which these foodstuffs, herbs and spices show after having eaten them. The medical science has developed following system: Every ingredient or herb has a directional effectiveness. Furthermore, there are herbs which have a special effect on certain organs.

The basic condition for a healthy metabolism is to obtain sufficient energy from food and that the digestive process doesn't use too much energy. An easily digestible meal makes content and sated, doesn't cause flatulence and fatigue after the meal. The perfect spices increase the healthiness of our meals. Very often, just small doses of herbs and spices will suffice. They are not used to make us sated, but to help our digestive organs to digest the food.

12.2 Recipes

The recipes list the ingredients to be used and the cooking instructions show how the dish is prepared. The list of ingredients shows the concerned quantities as well as the relevance for the therapy. If you find „less than mentioned", try to comply or find an alternative from the „list of recommended foodstuffs". Mostly it shall result just in a small change of taste when you simply avoid this ingredient.

Mild cooking methods: boiling, stewing, poaching, steaming
Strong cooking methods: barbecuing, roasting, frying, smoking
Balanced cooking methods: deep-frying, baking brick
Deep-freezing and warming in the microwave oven should be avoided (denaturalization).

12.3 Foodstuffs

Foodstuffs have an effect on body and soul like medicinal herbs, only a very much milder one. Dietary advice is mainly based on regional foodstuffs. The knowledge about the effects of each foodstuff and the knowledge, when which foodstuff shall be used, is based on the orthodox school of medicine. Use ecologic-organic products, if possible. As everything should be cooked for a long time due to a better digestability and very rarely eaten raw, the food agrees with everyone.

The classification of the foodstuffs according to their effect on the body is the basis in order to achieve a harmonious status of health.

Dietary advisors do not recommend certain foodstuffs for everyone. The individual diet is tailor-made for the individual constitution.

Buy only fresh and ripe fruit and vegetables. You ought to leave unripe fruit and vegetables and such with brown spots and wilted leaves behind in the market. In this case take deep-frozen goods (never ready-to-serve dishes!). Fruit and vegetables are deep-frozen immediately after harvesting and often contain more vitamins and minerals than the goods from the vegetable shelf. Whereas conserved or tinned goods contain very much less biological substances. Also, salt, sugar and others are mostly added to the latter. Never leave the foodstuffs in the water after washing them to avoid that many vital substances get drowned. Clean salads, fruit and vegetables immediately before serving.

Please make sure of the hygienic processing of foodstuffs. Clean your salads, fruit and vegetables carefully. When cooking with meat, prepare all ingredients first and then process the meat products. Clean the worktop and tools very carefully. Wooden surfaces ought to be treated with a mild disinfectant regularly in order to reduce germination.

Store fruit and vegetables separately, if possible. Harvested fruit and vegetables are still alive and emit e.g. ethylene gas, which makes other products ripen and age faster. Keep meat and fish in the closed packaging or store them in the fridge in closed containers.

12.4 Herbs

There are some basic rules for storing medicinal herbs. On principle, herbs must be protected from direct sunlight, humidity and heat.

Containers for the storage of herbs may be glasses, ceramic jars and even plastic containers. However, plastic is a rather unsuitable material and should only be a short-term solution. In case of glass containers, use a dark material.

Medicinal herbs cannot be kept for any long period. The shelf life of herbs is limited. However, it can be prolonged with suitable storage. The place should be dark, rather cool and absolutely dry. A wooden medicine cabinet, placed not directly next to a source of heat, would be ideal. Never buy large quantities of herbs so as not to have to throw them away. Label the container with the name of the herb and the date of harvesting or processing.

13 Other dietic-books

The following syndromes of dietetics, TCM or for a therapy supplement for cancer are available.

Dietetics

E001. Nutrition of the infant - baby food
E002. Nutrition during lactation
E003. Nutrition in old age
E004. Nutrition of children and adolescents
E005. Nutrition of athletes
E006. Light weight
E007. Pregnancy
E008. Full food

Protein and electrolyte - kidneys
E009. (hemodialysis) dialysis treatment
E010. Acute renal failure
E011. Chronic renal insufficiency
E012. Nephrotic syndrome
E013. Kidney stones (nephrolithiasis)

Gastrointestinal tract - pancreas
E014. Acute pancreatitis (inflammation of the pancreas)
E015. Chronic pancreatitis (inflammation of the pancreas)

Gastrointestinal tract - small intestine and large intestine
E016. Acute obstipation (constipation)
E017. Chronic obstipation (constipation)
E018. Colon irritabile
E019. Diverticulitis
E020. Acquired lactose intolerance (lactose malabsorption)
E021. Fructose malabsorption
E022. Glutensensitive enteropathy (celiac disease)
E023. Colectomy
E024. Short Bowel Syndrome

Gastrointestinal tract - liver, gallbladder, bile ducts
E025. Acute and chronic hepatitis (inflammation of the liver)
E026. Cholelithiasis (bile stones)
E027. fatty liver
E028. cirrhosis

Gastrointestinal tract - Stomach and duodenal intestine
E029. Acute gastritis
E030. Chronic gastritis
E031. Stomach bleeding
E032. Ulcus ventriculi and duodenal ulcer
E033. Condition after gastric surgery

Gastrointestinal tract - oral cavity and esophagus
E034. Stomatitis
E035. Esophageal carcinoma (esophageal cancer)
E036. Refluosophagitis (heartburn)

Special diseases
E037. Phenylketonuria (PKU)
E038. Rheumatic joint diseases

Metabolism
E039. Obesity (overweight)
E040. Diabetes mellitus
E041. Eating disorders (underweight)

Fat metabolism
E042. Hypercholesterolaemia (increased cholesterol level)
E043. Hepatic Encephalopathy

Heart and circulation
E044. Arteriosclerosis (arterial calcification)
E045. Heart insufficiency
E046. Hypertension
E047. Hyperuricaemia and gout

Changed nutrient requirements
E048. In case of fever
E049. For malignant diseases
E050. After burns
E051. Radiation and chemotherapy

CANCER
E100. Pancreatic cancer
E101. Bladder cancer
E102. Blood cancer (leukemia)
E103. Breast cancer
E104. Colorectal cancer
E105. Gastric cancer
E106. Kidney cancer
E107. Esophageal cancer

TCM
E200. Bladder - moisture heat in the bladder
E201. Bladder - moisture and cold in the bladder
E202. Bladder - emptiness and cold in the bladder
E203. Large intestine - external cold affects the large intestine
E204. Large intestine - moisture heat in the large intestine
E205. Large intestine - heat blocks the intestine II acute
E206. Large intestine - dryness of the colon
E207. Large intestine - Yang deficiency (cold)
E208. Heart - Blood insufficiency
E209. Heart - Blood stagnation
E210. Heart - Fire
E211. Heart - Hot mucus clogs the heart pores

E212. Heart - Cold mucus clogs the heart pores
E213. Heart - Qi deficiency
E214. Heart - Yang deficiency
E215. Heart - Yin deficiency
E216. Liver - Ascending Liver Yang
E217. Liver - Blood deficiency
E218. Liver - Blood stagnation
E219. Liver - Moisture heat in liver and gall bladder
E220. Liver - Fire
E221. Liver - Gall bladder Qi-Empty
E222. Liver - Cold in the liver meridian
E223. Liver - Qi stagnation
E224. Liver - Wind
E225. Liver - Wind with ascending liver Yang
E226. Liver - Wind with blood anemic
E227. Liver - Wind with extreme heat
E228. Lung - Qi deficiency
E229. Lung - Mucus-moisture in the lungs
E230. Lung - Mucus-heat in the lungs
E231. Lung - Mucus-cold in the lungs
E232. Lung - Dryness of the lungs
E233. Lung - Wind-heat attacks the lungs
E234. Lung - Wind-cold affects the lungs
E235. Lung - Yin deficiency
E236. Stomach - Bloodstagnation
E237. Stomach - Fire
E238. Stomach - Cold with liquid
E239. Stomach - Nutrition stagnation
E240. Stomach - Qi deficiency
E241. Stomach - Rebellious Qi
E242. Stomach - Yin Emptiness
E243. Spleen - Heat and moisture attack the spleen
E244. Spleen - Coldness and moisture affects the spleen
E245. Spleen - Qi deficiency
E246. Spleen - Qi deficiency + Declining spleen Qi
E247. Spleen - Qi deficiency + spleen does not control the blood
E248. Spleen - Yang deficiency
E249. Kidney - Heart and kidney no longer communicate
E250. Kidney - Jing deficiency
E251. Kidney - Kidneys cannot receive the Qi
E252. Kidney - Qi is not stable
E253. Kidney - Yang deficiency
E254. Kidney - Yin deficiency

For further information visit di-book.com.

14 EBNS - Software for nutritional counseling

The main task of the database is to create personalized nutritional advice for each patient individually. The database was developed for Dietetics

and Traditional Chinese Medicine.
The Database supports training and advices in the daily work routine.

The computer program provides lists of recipes, ingredients and herbs, which are given to the client. individually adjustable according to patient's request from whole food to vegetarians (lacto, ovo, ...). For every register there is an information sheet which can be given to the client. All texts can be individually designed.

The syndromes can be combined and result in an intersection of the recommended recipes and ingredients. The automated diagnosis for the TCM enables you to check your experience during the training as well as to confirm your diagnosis in the working day. You select several predefined symptoms and have the program automatically display the relevant syndromes.

How to work with the database:
Select the patient / client, select one or more of the syndromes you diagnosed and print the folder.

You can change all values, create new symptoms or syndromes, develop recipes, change or adapt ingredients and herbs to your findings. In simple client management, all relevant data about the person is stored. You get an overview of the past diagnoses and the development of the course of the disease.

As a consultant you save a lot of time when you print out the recipe, food and herbal lists for the recognized syndromes and give them to the clients. You can use this time for a personal conversation. With the database, dieticians and nutritionists can view the nutrients and trace elements for each recipe and develop recipes for syndromes even with suggested ingredients.

All recipe and grocery lists can also be ordered from me as a combination of several diseases. I wish all readers good luck, health and happiness in life.
More information can be found at www.ebns.at.
Volunteer: www.krebsinfo.at
Josef Miligui